Please use this book to write, draw, and doodle

HELLO
my name is

Copyright © 2016 Emmett B. Kelly
All rights reserved.

ISBN: 1506132936
ISBN 13: 9781506132938
Library of Congress Control Number: 2016902637
LCCN My Sister Got Cancer: Daniel Island, South Carolina

My Sister Got Cancer

A Workbook for Siblings of Cancer Patients

Emmett B Kelly

My name is Emmett and I am nine years old. I have a little sister who is four. We are like most kids you know. We live with our mommy and daddy near Chicago. We like doing things as a family like playing together and taking family vacations. Last year at the beginning of school, my sister got **cancer**. My pa and I are writing this book to tell what it is like to have a sibling with cancer.

Cancer

My mommy is a nurse. She knows about cancer. She told me a lot about cancer when my sister got it. Cancer is when cells multiply too fast. When cells grow too fast, they can go out of control. When they go out of control, they can make kids very sick. This means that cancer is a serious disease. When someone gets cancer, they have to go to special doctors and go through special treatments. These treatments help get rid of the cancer.

Mommy says that there are lots of kinds of cancer. Some people get cancer when they are old, like my granny and pa. Other people get cancer when they are little, like my sister. When old people get cancer, their special treatments are different from the treatments for little kids. This is because they are older and they respond differently to the treatment. Most of the time, little kids do better than old people when their cancer is treated.

There are special doctors who help people with cancer. These doctors are called **oncologists.** They know all about cancer. They also know how to make it go away. My sister goes to an oncologist who only takes care of people with her kind of cancer. Her doctor gives her medicine every week. It keeps her cancer from growing more. The medicine her doctor gives her is called **chemotherapy.** Chemotherapy is a medication that gets rid of cancer cells. Sometimes it gets rid of all the cancer cells. Sometimes it only keeps them from growing. Doctors give people the right kind of medication for the cancer they have.

The doctor has to figure out what kind of cancer someone has before they know what kind of medication to give the patient. Sometimes they do this by taking some of the cancer cells out of the body. This is called a **biopsy**. The doctor uses a needle or a knife to take cells out of the body. Then he sends the cells to another doctor. This doctor is called a pathologist. The **pathologist** tells the oncologist what kind of cancer the person has. This helps the oncologist decide what medication will get rid of the cancer.

There are other ways to get rid of cancer cells. One way is with **surgery**, where a doctor, called a **surgeon**, takes the cancer out of the body. Another doctor makes kids comfortable while they are having surgery. This doctor is called an **anesthesiologist**. Surgeons and anesthesiologists always work together to make sure kids are OK while having surgery. Some kinds of cancer can be completely cured with surgery.

Some cancer cells are removed by radiation. This is called **radiation therapy**. A special doctor aims a special light right at the cancer cells to get rid of them. This kind of doctor is called a **radiation oncologist**. The radiation oncologist studies cancer in the body and makes a plan for removing it with radiation. Radiation does not hurt. The treatment is over very quickly. However, kids who get radiation therapy have to go to the hospital every school day. Most of the time, they have to go for a few weeks.

Doctors always want to get rid of as many cancer cells as they can. Cancer doctors get rid of the cells in different ways. My sister had surgery to cut out the cancer cells. She also had chemotherapy to get rid of any cells that might have been left. She also had radiation therapy to get rid of any cells that were still left after having chemotherapy. The doctors really blasted that cancer.

Questions ✶ ✶ ✶

✶ Why do kids get cancer?
No one knows why kids get cancer. What we do know is that they do not get it from other kids, or from adults.

✶ Can I get cancer from someone else?
No way! Cancer is not like a cold or a sore throat. You cannot get cancer from someone else. If you have cancer, you cannot give it to someone else.

✶ Did kids with cancer do something bad that gave them cancer?
Absolutely not! There is nothing a kid can do to keep from getting cancer. There is nothing a kid can do to get cancer. No one knows what causes cancer. We do know that it is not caused by something that a kid or their family did.

✶ Does cancer hurt?
Cancer often does not hurt. Sometimes it can hurt a little or a lot. Many times the treatments for cancer make kids tired. Also, sometimes the treatments make kids sick to their stomachs or their food not taste good.

Work Pages

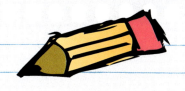

I got scared when my sister got cancer. What scared me most was not knowing what was going to happen to her.

Are you scared about your brother or sister getting cancer? What is most scary to you? Write or draw a picture.

When I first found out that my sister had cancer, I was scared by what my mommy was telling me about cancer. When my sister started getting treatments, I wasn't scared anymore.

Were you more scared before your brother or sister got treatments than after they began? Write or draw a picture.

My mommy is really good at explaining stuff to my sister and me. She even tells us when something is going to hurt for a count of five or ten. Do you have someone who is good at explaining stuff to you? Who is that? Write or draw a picture.

I felt better after my sister was finished with her first treatment. It wasn't so bad.

How did you feel about the treatments after they were started? Write or draw a picture.

My mommy cries sometimes. She pretends that she has something in her eye, but I know she is crying.

Do you know an adult who cries because of cancer? How does that make you feel? Write or draw a picture.

Treatments

Some kids get one kind of treatment to get rid of their cancer. Other kids get two kinds. My sister had three kinds of treatment. Some treatments last a few weeks. Other treatments can last for months or even years. My sister's treatments lasted almost a year.

During treatment, my sister was a little different than before she got cancer. Sometimes, she did not have much energy. She sat around more than usual and watched TV. She even took naps. My sister never took naps before she got cancer. It was weird seeing her sleep during the daytime.

Also, my sister sometimes got sick to her stomach. This usually happened right after her treatments. She said that food tasted funny, and she didn't want to eat. Sometimes my mommy gave her a plastic spoon instead of the spoons the rest of us used at dinner. That helped the food taste better. Sometimes she let my sister have whatever she wanted to eat, even ice cream. She even gave her ice cream at lunch when she didn't eat her sandwich first.

My sister went bald from the chemotherapy. It never bothered my sister to be bald. Kids asked me why she was bald. I told them that the medicine she was taking made her that way and that her hair would come back after she was finished with the medicine. My sister wore a hat most of the time when she went outside. She almost never wore a hat in the house. Everybody knew that my sister was bald. I didn't always like that.

My parents were different when my sister was getting treatments. My mommy always went to the hospital with her. My daddy still took me to school and came home in time for dinner. I didn't like it when my mommy had to be with my sister and not with me. Sometimes I went to the hospital to be with my sister and my mommy. I liked doing that. The people at the hospital were very nice to my sister. They were nice to me, too. They brought toys and stuff for both of us to play with when we were there.

Questions ✶ ✶ ✶

✶ **Do all kids with cancer go bald?**
Not every kid with cancer goes bald. It depends on the treatment they have to get rid of their cancer cells. However, many kids do go bald when they are treated for cancer. Their hair grows back when the treatments are over.

✶ **Why do kids with cancer get so many treatments?**
Cancer is a serious illness. Doctors want to make sure every single cancer cell is gone. Sometimes this means that they do extra treatments to make sure all the cells are gone.

✶ **Do kids with cancer go to school?**
Most of the time, kids with cancer go to school. Sometimes they may miss some days, but mostly they go like everyone else.

* **How long does it take for kids with cancer to get better?**
That depends on the kind of cancer a kid has. Sometimes a kid gets better in just a few weeks. Other times it takes a long time. There are many kinds of cancer. Therefore, there are many ways to treat it.

* **Should I be afraid of a kid with cancer?**
No way! They are just like every other kid. They have to go through treatments to get better. They cannot hurt you with their cancer. You cannot hurt them unless you are mean to them.

* **Can kids with cancer go on vacation?**
Sure, they can do most anything they feel like doing. Sometimes they are a little too tired to run as much as other kids. There are special vacation camps for kids with cancer. They are really cool places where kids with cancer can get together for summer camp.

Work Pages

I thought it wasn't fair when my sister got treats without eating her meal and I had to eat regular food before getting a treat.

Did you have anything happen to you that you thought was not fair? If so, what? Write or draw a picture.

My mommy paid a lot more attention to my sister than to me. I missed having my mommy's attention.
Did you miss getting someone's attention? If so, how did it make you feel? Write or draw a picture.

My sister is always getting toys and gifts from other people. I almost never get a gift, too. I think this is not fair, but I never say what I think about it.

If your brother or sister gets more stuff than you, how does it make you feel? Write or draw a picture.

My sister sometimes pitches fits that I know are fake, but she gets her way.

Does your brother or sister ever get their way by pitching fake fits? How does that make you feel? Write or draw a picture.

Sometimes my grandma and grandpa or aunt and uncle take me to things like karate and piano when I would rather have my mommy or daddy take me.
If your parents ever ask someone else to take you where they used to go with you, how does that make you feel?
Write or draw a picture.

My daddy always puts us to bed, just like he did before my sister got cancer. I like that.

What are some special things your family did before your brother or sister got cancer that you still do? Write or draw a picture.

I am proud of my sister. She has done a good job fighting her cancer. I tell her she does a good job.

Are you proud of your brother or sister? Have you ever told them that you are proud of them? Write or draw a picture.

My sister comes to my baseball games, even when she is tired. I like it that she comes.

Does your brother or sister do things for you, even though they are tired? How does that make you feel? Write or draw a picture.

What People Say

Most people know my sister has cancer. My family and our friends know because Mommy and Daddy told them. My friends at school know because they have seen my sister's bald head and have asked me what is wrong with her. Even strangers know because of her bald head. It is hard not to notice a bald kid.

Most of the time, people say nice stuff to us about my sister. They say things like, "What can I do to help?" or "Feel free to call us anytime." Some people say that they are praying special prayers for my sister.

People also say how cute my sister looks with her bald head. They say she has cute clothes. They say she looks adorable. My sister likes

to show off her clothes. She dresses up like a princess and goes everywhere in her dress-up clothes. When she dresses like a princess, she wears a crown. Sometimes she wears a hat to keep her head warm, but not all the time.

I wish people didn't know so much about my sister's cancer. Kids ask questions like, "What happened to your sister?" I say, "She got cancer." I would rather just be like other kids whose sisters don't have cancer. No one asks about their sisters.

Adults sometimes look at us funny. When we go to church or to the grocery store, people look at my sister. It is hard to have a bald sister.

Questions ✱ ✱ ✱

✱ **Why do people say special prayers for kids with cancer?**
Cancer is a serious disease that takes a long time to treat. It is hard for a kid with cancer to have the treatments. Just like other kids, kids with cancer would rather be doing other things than getting treated for cancer. It is good to say special prayers for kids with cancer. It is not easy for them.

✱ **What should I say to a kid who has cancer?**
Kids with cancer are just like any other kids. They are interested in exactly the same things that every other kid cares about. You can ask the kid to tell you about the cancer if you want. However, kids with cancer simply want to be treated like everyone else.

✱ **Why do people always look funny at kids who are bald?**
People are not used to seeing kids with cancer. They are sorry that they got sick. They want to help kids with cancer, but they don't know how. They are being nice when they look. They do not mean to make you uncomfortable.

✱ **What should I say to kids who ask what is wrong with my brother or sister?**
Simply say that they got cancer. You can also say that their hair will grow back when they stop getting the medicine.

✱ **What if someone says something mean?**
If someone says or does something mean, walk away from them. Then go tell your mommy or daddy what they said. You can talk about it.

Work Pages

My friends at school know that my sister has cancer, and they ask me questions about it that make me feel different.

Have other kids ever said stuff to you that made you feel uncomfortable? If so, what? Write or draw a picture.

Sometimes when my sister takes off her hat, everyone sees her bald head. This makes me feel that our family is different.

Has anything ever happened to make you feel that your family is different from others? If so, what? Write or draw a picture.

Sometimes there are too many people around our house. I would rather just be alone with my mommy and daddy and sister.
If there are ever too many people around, does that bother you? Write or draw a picture.

Adults talk about my sister when they think I am not around. This makes me think they are hiding stuff from me.
If that has happened to you, how did it make you feel? Write or draw a picture.

Vocabulary Words

Hospitals and doctors and nurses use words that most of us do not understand. Here is a list of vocabulary words that can help you understand what they are talking about. There are many different doctors who help kids with cancer:

Anesthesiologist (an-es-thē-zē-ä-lə-jist): a doctor who makes people comfortable when they are having surgery or tests.

Surgeon (sər-jən): a doctor who operates on people.

Oncologist (än-kä-lə-jist): a doctor who takes care of people with cancer.

Pathologist (pə-thä-lə-jist): a doctor who studies blood and tissues with microscopes and other instruments.

Radiation oncologist (rā-dē-ā-shen än-kä-lə-jist): a doctor who gets rid of cancer cells by using beams of radiation.

Radiologist (rā-dē-ä-lə-jist): a doctor who studies images taken with X-ray machines and scanning devices.

There are lots of words that describe how diseases are found:

Biopsy (bī-äp-sē): when a doctor takes a piece of tissue out of someone to test it in the laboratory.

Cancer (kan[t]-sər): cells that grow too fast and cause problems.

CT scanner (C T ska-ner): a machine that looks like a huge doughnut and that takes a picture of the inside of someone's body.

Diagnosis (dī-ig-nō-səs): when doctors identify what is wrong with someone after examining their symptoms.

Malignancy (mə-lignəsē): a cell or group of cells that is made of cancer.

Mass (mas): a group of cells that is where it is not supposed to be.

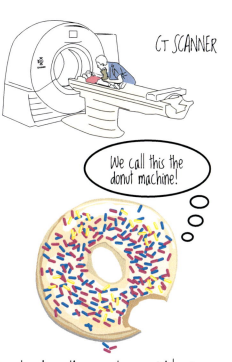

Monitor (mä-nə-tər): a machine that keeps track of things like someone's heart rate, breathing rate, and blood pressure.

Symptom (sim[p]-təm): a problem that tells doctors that something is wrong with someone.

Tissue (ti-shü): a group of cells.

Tumor (tü-mər): a group of cells that is bunched together in a place where they don't belong.

Ultrasound (əl-trə-saúnd): a machine that takes a moving picture of the inside of someone's body.

There are words that describe treatments for cancer:

Anesthesia (a-nəs-thē-zhə): what a doctor uses to make someone comfortable during surgery.

Blood transfusion (bləd tran[t]s-fyü-zhən): when a person gets someone else's blood through an IV to make them stronger.

Chemotherapy (che-mo-ther-ə-pē): when someone gets medicine to get rid of cancer cells.

Fluid (flü-əd): fancy water that is put into someone's body to make them better.

IV (I V): a tube with a needle that goes from a bag of fluid to someone's arm or port.

Operating room (ä-pə-rāt-ing rüm): a room in the hospital where doctors do surgery.

Port (pórt): a small button that the doctor puts under someone's skin to hold a needle for an IV.

Radiation therapy (rā-dē-ā-shen ther-ə-pē): when a technician shoots a beam of radiation at cancer cells.

Recovery room (ri-kə-və-rē rüm): a room in the hospital where people go to wake up after getting an anesthetic.

Side effect (sīd i-fekt): a symptom that happens when people are given treatments to help them get rid of cancer or some other disease. Feeling sick or tired, vomiting, or having a fever are sometimes side effects of cancer treatment.

Surgery (sərj-rē): when a person gets something cut out of their body or has something fixed in their body by a doctor.

Afterward

Approximately 1 in 315 children in the United States will develop cancer before the age of 15. The cancers that children typically develop differ from those that occur in adults. The most common childhood cancer is leukemia. Others include brain tumors, lymphomas, neuroblastoma, Wilms' tumors, and sarcomas such as rhabdomyosarcoma and osteosarcoma. For the most part, causes of childhood cancers remain unclear, but it is known that changes in genes that promote the growth and survival of cells are usually present in predictable patterns for different types of cancer. Today, we can identify many of the genetic changes that are present in childhood cancer cells. We hope that in the near future this information will provide us with a better understanding of why children develop cancer and will lead to new treatment approaches for childhood cancer.

Fortunately, the cure rate for children and young adults with cancer has improved dramatically during the past fifty years. Much of the improvement can be attributed to the introduction of chemotherapy to surgery and radiotherapy. Most importantly, treatment regimens have been systematically tested through clinical trials and the results have been reported, so we have been able to efficiently build upon past success. Intensification of treatment regimens has contributed to the improved cure rate and became possible, in part, because of new supportive care measures, which allow patients to tolerate more intensive treatment with fewer immediate side effects. Depending on the type of cancer, treatment may last a few months to three years and involve visits to clinics and sometimes hospital admissions. It may also be necessary to take medication on a daily basis. Of course, diagnosis and treatment have a tremendous impact on the children and their families, including the patients' siblings, who may not be able to or know how to express all of their concerns. This book addresses questions and concerns that may arise in the mind of a child whose sibling has cancer. I believe it will be of great interest to families who have been affected by childhood cancer, as well as others. I thank the Brown/Kelly family for their ongoing commitment to children with cancer.

David Walterhouse, MD

All proceeds from this book go to the research efforts of the Pediatric Oncofertility Research Foundation (www.porf.org)

Made in the USA
Monee, IL
16 February 2021